YOUR ONLY LIMIT IS YOU

summersdale

An Hachette UK Company
www.hachette.co.uk

Summersdale Publishers
Part of Octopus Publishing Group Limited
Carmelite House
50 Victoria Embankment
LONDON
EC4Y 0DZ
UK

www.summersdale.com

The authorized representative in the EEA is Hachette Ireland, 8 Castlecourt Centre, Dublin 15, D15 XTP3, Ireland (email: info@hbgi.ie)

Printed and bound in China

ISBN: 978-1-83799-830-2
eISBN: 978-1-83799-831-9

This FSC® label means that materials and other controlled sources used for the product have been responsibly sourced

MIX
Paper | Supporting responsible forestry
FSC® C016973

Substantial discounts on bulk quantities of Summersdale books are available to corporations, professional associations and other organizations. For details contact general enquiries: telephone: +44 (0) 1243 771107 or email: enquiries@summersdale.com.

To.....................................

From.................................

Nothing is worth more than this day.

JOHANN WOLFGANG
VON GOETHE

Anything can be achieved
with a good, healthy
dose of courage.

Viola Davis

TODAY IS THE ONLY DAY IN WHICH WE HAVE ANY POWER.

Steve Maraboli

FOLLOW
-YOUR-
DREAMS

Never give up then,
for that is just the
place and time
that the tide will turn.

HARRIET BEECHER STOWE

We are the change that we seek.

BARACK OBAMA

My vision for
my career is too
precious to let
loose among
the naysayers.
Don't feed
your dreams
to the lions.

BERNARDINE EVARISTO

GOOD DAYS START WITH GOOD THOUGHTS

Don't ever doubt
yourselves or waste
a second of your life.

ARIANA GRANDE

"

ERRORS...
ARE THE PORTALS
OF DISCOVERY.

James Joyce

"

Nothing really matters except what you do now in this instant of time.

EILEEN CADDY

JUST KEEP GOING!

The question
isn't who is going
to let me;
it's who is going
to stop me.

Ayn Rand

It's character traits like persistence, ambition, inquisitiveness and grit that will determine your success.

AMAL CLOONEY

CHALLENGE YOURSELF; IT'S THE ONLY PATH WHICH LEADS TO GROWTH.

Morgan Freeman

YOU'RE EITHER WINNING -OR- LEARNING

Always go with your passions. Never ask yourself if it's realistic or not.

DEEPAK CHOPRA

It's only when you
risk failure that you
discover things.

LUPITA NYONG'O

It's never too late – never too late to start over, never too late to be happy.

JANE FONDA

TAKE
SMALL
STEPS
EVERY
DAY

"

TRY AND FAIL,
BUT NEVER
FAIL TO TRY!

Jared Leto

The man who removes a mountain begins by carrying away small stones.

CHINESE PROVERB

We're all capable of climbing so much higher than we usually permit ourselves to suppose.

OCTAVIA E. BUTLER

KEEP YOUR EYES ON THE PRIZE

YOU GET WHATEVER ACCOMPLISHMENT YOU ARE WILLING TO DECLARE.

Georgia O'Keeffe

I don't think limits.

USAIN BOLT

Act as if what you do makes a difference. It does.

WILLIAM JAMES

GRAB LIFE WITH -BOTH- HANDS

We can put fear
of the future in
front of us to block
us or behind us to
drive us forward.

Michaela Coel

Don't wait. The time
will never be just right.

NAPOLEON HILL

There are two ways
you can get through pain.
You can let it destroy you,
or you can use it as fuel
to drive you: to dream
bigger, work harder.

Taylor Swift

SQUEEZE ALL THE JUICE OUT OF TODAY!

You can, you
should, and
if you're brave
enough to
start, you will.

STEPHEN KING

THERE ARE POSSIBILITIES ALL AROUND YOU – MAGIC ALL AROUND YOU – NO MATTER WHAT SITUATION YOU'RE IN.

Keke Palmer

Better to live one
year as a tiger, than a
hundred as a sheep.

MADONNA

DOORS
WERE
MADE
TO BE
OPENED

What would life be if we had no courage to attempt anything?

VINCENT VAN GOGH

**Life shrinks
or expands in
proportion to
one's courage.**

ANAÏS NIN

I DON'T GET BITTER, I JUST GET BETTER.

Rihanna

GIVE IT YOUR -BEST- SHOT!

LIFE IS A HELLUVA
LOT MORE FUN
IF YOU SAY YES
RATHER THAN NO.

Richard Branson

In the dark times, if you have something to hold on to, which is yourself, you'll survive.

WHOOPI GOLDBERG

EVERY
DAY IS
A NEW
CHANCE

Be brave and fearless
to know that even if
you do make a wrong
decision, you're making
it for a good reason.

Adele

BE LOUD ABOUT THE THINGS THAT ARE IMPORTANT TO YOU.

Karen Walrond

Procrastination
is opportunity's
natural assassin.

VICTOR KIAM

Change your life today. Don't gamble on the future, act now, without delay.

SIMONE DE BEAUVOIR

NEVER FORGET HOW FAR YOU'VE ALREADY COME

In life, you have ups and downs, but you should never give up. You should always try to get ahead.

YALITZA APARICIO

Don't be afraid to think outside the box. Don't be afraid to fail big, to dream big.

DENZEL WASHINGTON

YOU ARE
RIGHT
WHERE
-YOU-
NEED
TO BE

"

THE EXCITEMENT
OF DREAMS COMING
TRUE IS BEYOND THE
DESCRIPTION OF WORDS.

Lailah Gifty Akita

"

Be bold, be brave enough
to be your true self.

Queen Latifah

If you ask me
what I came into
this life to do,
I will tell you:
I came to
live out loud.

ÉMILE ZOLA

OPPORTUNITY DOES NOT KNOCK – IT PRESENTS ITSELF WHEN YOU BEAT DOWN THE DOOR.

Kyle Chandler

THE
BEST
TIME
TO START
IS NOW!

If you rest,
you rust.

HELEN HAYES

The more we do, the more we can do.

WILLIAM HAZLITT

Anyone can hide. Facing up to things, working through them, that's what makes you strong.

SARAH DESSEN

TAKE YOUR DREAMS SERIOUSLY

Be fearless, be brave,
be bold, love yourself.

HARUKI MURAKAMI

"

JUST DON'T GIVE UP
TRYING TO DO
WHAT YOU REALLY
WANT TO DO.

Ella Fitzgerald

So what are you afraid of? What is holding you back? What is it that stands in your way? Do it!

NORMAN VINCENT PEALE

YOU
ARE THE
HERO OF
YOUR
STORY

Don't ask yourself
what the world needs.
Ask yourself what
makes you come
alive and then
go do that.

Howard Thurman

Don't be afraid to look silly. You are only holding yourself back if you are afraid of looking silly or failing.

AISLING BEA

SHOOT
FOR THE
STARS!

IF I CAN CREATE
THE MINIMUM OF
MY PLANS AND
DESIRES THERE
SHALL BE NO
REGRETS.

Bessie
Coleman

Do what you can, with what you've got, where you are.

THEODORE ROOSEVELT

The beginning is always today.

MARY SHELLEY

YOU ARE POWERFUL AND BRAVE

Don't let success get
to your head or failure
get to your heart.

ANTHONY JOSHUA

FOREVER –
IS COMPOSED
OF NOWS.

Emily Dickinson

YOU
-CAN-
DO IT

Each and every one of us is amazing in our own way.

NORMANI

Hope lies in dreams,
in imagination and
in the courage of those
who dare to make
dreams into reality.

Jonas Salk

I HAVE MY FLAWS, BUT I EMBRACE THEM AND I LOVE THEM BECAUSE THEY'RE MINE.

Winnie Harlow

GOOD THINGS COME TO THOSE WHO HUSTLE!

Life isn't about finding
yourself. Life is about
creating yourself.

GEORGE BERNARD SHAW

Don't sit
down and
wait for the
opportunities
to come.
Get up and
make them.

MADAM C. J. WALKER

You are never
too old to set
another goal
or to dream
a new dream.

LES BROWN

WHAT WILL YOU DO TODAY?

You must never be
fearful about what you
are doing when it is right.

ROSA PARKS

"

IF I AM NOT FOR
MYSELF, WHO WILL
BE FOR ME... AND
IF NOT NOW, WHEN?

Hillel the Elder

"

There is nothing impossible to him who will try.

Alexander the Great

GOOD VIBES
-ONLY-

Life is either
a daring
adventure
or nothing.

HELEN KELLER

OPPORTUNITIES MULTIPLY AS THEY ARE SEIZED.

Sun Tzu

You have to have
confidence in your
ability, and then be
tough enough
to follow through.

ROSALYNN CARTER

Keep your eyes on the finish line and not on the turmoil around you.

RIHANNA

Things do not happen. Things are made to happen.

JOHN F. KENNEDY

YOU CAN
NEVER FAIL
AS LONG
AS YOU GET
BACK UP AGAIN

The mind is everything. If you don't believe you can do something, then you can't.

KAI GREENE

NEVER
GIVE
UP

"

INSTEAD OF LETTING
YOUR HARDSHIPS AND
FAILURES DISCOURAGE
OR EXHAUST YOU,
LET THEM INSPIRE YOU.

Michelle Obama

Opportunity is missed by most people because it is dressed in overalls and looks like work.

THOMAS EDISON

Never ever refer
to yourself as "lucky"...
you worked for this.
Take the credit.
Absorb the praise.
Dance in the light.
This was ALL you.

Chidera Eggerue

DON'T WORRY ABOUT - THE - HATERS

YOU CAN'T EXPECT TO HIT THE JACKPOT IF YOU DON'T PUT A FEW NICKELS IN THE MACHINE.

Flip Wilson

Tomorrow is promised
to no one. Prioritize
today accordingly.

GINA GREENLEE

It does not matter how slowly you go as long as you do not stop.

CONFUCIUS

**SHOW
THE WORLD
WHAT YOU'RE
MADE OF!**

If everything
was perfect,
you would
never learn
and you would
never grow.

BEYONCÉ

I'd rather regret
the things I've done
than regret the things
I haven't done.

LUCILLE BALL

"

OPPORTUNITIES
ARE LIKE SUNRISES.
IF YOU WAIT TOO LONG,
YOU MISS THEM.

William Arthur Ward

TAKE A DEEP BREATH AND GO FOR IT!

If there's a book you want to read, but it hasn't been written yet, then you must write it.

TONI MORRISON

You can't be that
kid standing at the
top of the waterslide,
overthinking it.
You have to go
down the chute.

Tina Fey

ONLY THOSE
WHO WILL RISK
GOING TOO
FAR CAN
POSSIBLY FIND
OUT HOW FAR
ONE CAN GO.

T. S.
Eliot

DON'T STOP UNTIL
- YOU'RE -
PROUD

Step through new doors. The majority of the time there's something fantastic on the other side.

OPRAH WINFREY

You have to stop crying, and you have to go kick some ass.

LADY GAGA

Life begins at the end of your comfort zone.

NEALE DONALD WALSCH

**BETTER
AN "OOPS"
THAN A
"WHAT IF"**

Put all excuses aside
and remember this:
YOU are capable.

ZIG ZIGLAR

"

YOU HAVE TO
BELIEVE IN YOURSELF
WHEN NO ONE ELSE
DOES – THAT MAKES
YOU A WINNER
RIGHT THERE.

Venus Williams

"

DON'T WISH FOR IT – WORK FOR IT

One may walk over the highest mountain one step at a time.

JOHN WANAMAKER

Hope is not
something
that you have.
Hope is something
that you create
with your actions.

Alexandria Ocasio-Cortez

The purpose of life is to live it, to taste experience to the utmost, to reach out eagerly and without fear for newer and richer experience.

ELEANOR ROOSEVELT

DON'T DREAM OF WINNING. TRAIN FOR IT.

Mo Farah

Waking up in truth is so much better than living in a lie.

IDRIS ELBA

I am not lucky.
You know what
I am? I am smart,
I am talented,
I take advantage of
the opportunities
that come my way...
Don't call me lucky.
Call me a badass.

SHONDA RHIMES

NOTHING CAN STOP A DETERMINED -HEART-

Find something you're
passionate about
and keep tremendously
interested in it.

JULIA CHILD

66

IF YOU CAN
DREAM IT, YOU
CAN DO IT.

Tom Fitzgerald

I feel like people are expecting me to fail, therefore, I expect myself to win.

LEWIS HAMILTON

Perseverance
is failing nineteen
times and succeeding
the twentieth.

Julie Andrews

GO FOR IT NOW. THE FUTURE IS PROMISED TO NO ONE.

Wayne Dyer

YOU'VE
TOTALLY
GOT THIS

You're brilliant, you know that. You can achieve anything you put your mind to.

JESSICA ENNIS-HILL

Boldness be my friend.

WILLIAM SHAKESPEARE

**Take that
big leap
forward without
hesitation,
without once
looking back.**

ALYSON NOËL

Success is not achieved
by winning all the time.
Real success comes when
we rise after we fall.

MUHAMMAD ALI

DREAM BIG, WORK HARD, STAY FOCUSED

WE ALWAYS
MAY BE
WHAT WE
MIGHT HAVE
BEEN.

Adelaide Anne Procter

Don't be afraid
to push the
boundaries.

PAULA RADCLIFFE

The struggles
along the way
are only meant
to shape you
for your purpose.

Chadwick Boseman

NOTHING IS IMPOSSIBLE. THE WORD ITSELF SAYS "I'M POSSIBLE!"

Audrey Hepburn

Being realistic is the
most commonly
travelled road
to mediocrity.

WILL SMITH

GO
ALL
IN

Make bold choices and make mistakes. It's all those things that add up to the person you become.

ANGELINA JOLIE

Tell me, what is it
you plan to do with
your one wild and
precious life?

MARY OLIVER

No matter what
people tell you,
words and ideas
can change
the world.

ROBIN WILLIAMS

MAKE IT HAPPEN

YOU ARE ON
THE EVE OF A
COMPLETE VICTORY.
YOU CAN'T GO WRONG.
THE WORLD IS
BEHIND YOU.

Josephine Baker

Live your own
life, and follow
your own star.

WILFERD PETERSON

You have to wake
up every day and say,
"There's no reason
today can't be the
best day of my life."

Blake Lively

JUST SAY "YIKES" AND MOVE ON

YOU MAY NOT
CONTROL ALL
THE EVENTS THAT
HAPPEN TO YOU,
BUT YOU CAN
DECIDE NOT
TO BE REDUCED
BY THEM.

Maya
Angelou

Wherever you are,
be all there.

JIM ELLIOT

It's my purpose
to just shine a
light where I can,
do something
where I can, just
whatever I can,
in whatever way,
shape or form.

STORMZY

SOMETIMES,
WHAT YOU'RE
LOOKING FOR IS
ALREADY THERE.

Aretha Franklin

ONE DAY, OR DAY ONE – IT'S UP TO YOU

I can,
therefore
I am.

SIMONE WEIL

YOUR
ONLY
LIMIT
-IS-
YOU

Have you enjoyed this book? If so, find us on Facebook at **Summersdale Publishers**, on Twitter/X at **@Summersdale** and on Instagram, TikTok and Bluesky at **@summersdalebooks** and get in touch. We'd love to hear from you!

www.summersdale.com